Just Sweethearts

Polar bears © Frans Lanting / Minden Pictures

Just Sweethearts

Wild thoughts about love

compiled by
Bonnie Louise Kuchler

Published by Willow Creek Press
P.O. Box 147, Minocqua, Wisconsin 54548

Design: Pat Linder
Editor: Andrea Donner

Library of Congress Cataloging-in-Publication Data
Just sweethearts : "wild" thoughts about love / compiled by Bonnie Louise Kuchler.
p. cm.
ISBN 1-57223-688-4 (hard : alk. paper)
1. Love--Quotations, maxims, etc. 2. Animals--Pictorial works. I. Kuchler, Bonnie Louise, 1958-
PN6084.L6 J87 2003
302.3--dc21

2002154110

Printed in Canada

©Len Rue, Jr.

For Phillip, my husband, best friend, and pillow

Acknowledgements

Thanks to my husband for his unwavering, shamelessly uninhibited promotion of my books. Thanks to my mom for saying this is my best yet. Thanks to Jill, Nate, Laura and Denise for second, third, fourth, and fifth opinions on which pictures to use. And humble thanks to the whole gang at Willow Creek Press—especially to Tom, Andrea, Pat, Jeremy, and Page—for working so hard on my dreams.

Once in a while,
right in the middle of an ordinary life,
love gives us a fairy tale.

UNKNOWN AUTHOR

Moose © Ron Sanford / Alaska Stock Images

There is no surprise more magical than the surprise of being loved.

CHARLES MORGAN
English writer

Hippopotamus © Art Wolfe/www.artwolfe.com

Love is the enchanted dawn
of every heart.

ALPHONSE DE LAMARTINE
French poet and statesman

Swans © Richard Bowsher / Nature Picture Library

*If it is your time,
love will track you down
like a cruise missile.*

LYNDA BARRY
American cartoonist, writer

Bald eagles © Bill Silliker, Jr.

A man falls in love through his eyes,
a woman through her ears.

WOODROW WYATT
British journalist

Young goats © Hans Reinhard / BCIUSA

A kiss . . .
'Tis a secret told to the mouth
instead of to the ear.

EDMOND ROSTAND
French playwright

Prairie dogs © Tom & Pat Leeson

*At the touch of love,
everyone becomes a poet.*

PLATO

Wolverine kits © Daniel J. Cox / Natural Exposures, Inc.

Love is a peculiar thing.

GEORG BUCHNER
German dramatist, revolutionary

Giraffes © International Stock / ImageState, Inc.

There is nothing like desire
for preventing the things one says
from bearing any resemblance
to what one has in mind.

MARCEL PROUST
French novelist

Greater flamingoes © M. Watson / Ardea London

Love is like an hourglass,
with the heart filling up
as the brain empties.

JULES RENARD
French dramatist and author

Marine iguanas © Michio Hoshino / Minden Pictures

*The first sigh of love
is the last of wisdom.*

French proverb

Western grey kangaroos © Howie Garber / Wanderlust Images

Love at first sight is easy to understand. It's when two people have been looking at each other for years that it becomes a miracle.

SAM LEVENSON
American humorist

Black Crowned Herons © Dale Sweeney / Image State

Love is a great beautifier.

LOUISA MAY ALCOTT
American author

Marine iguanas © Mark Jones / Minden Pictures

Love is like wildflowers.
It is often found in the
most unlikely places.

H. Jackson Brown
American author

Raccoons © Daniel J. Cox / Natural Exposures, Inc.

There's always room for love;
you just have to move a few things around.

UNKNOWN AUTHOR

Hippopotamuses © Steve Solum / BCIUSA

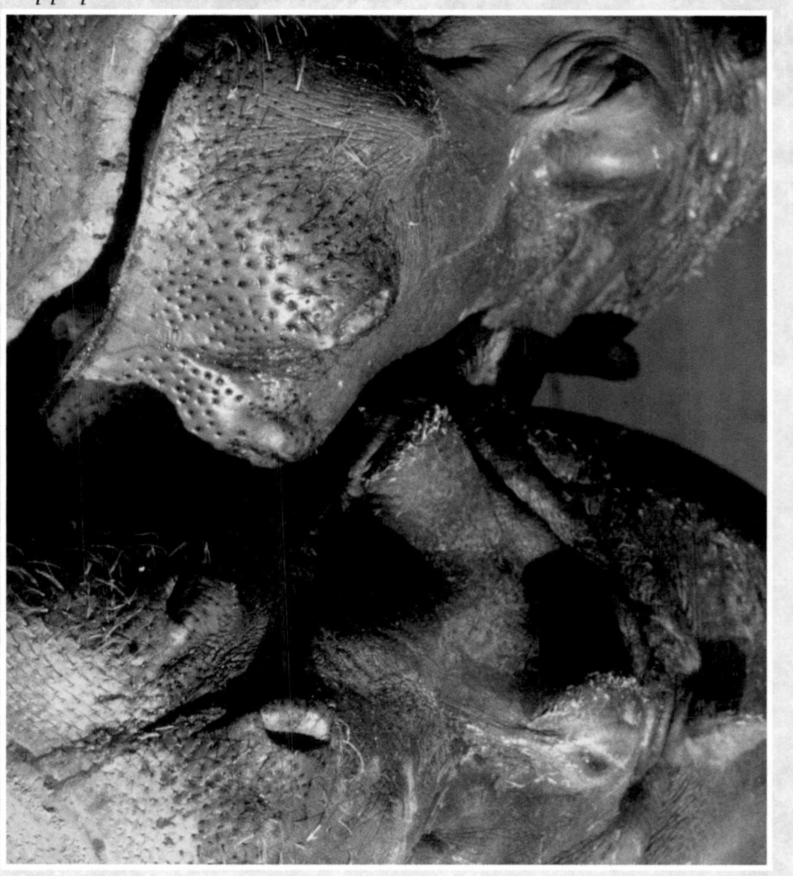

Love is like a butterfly.
It goes where it pleases,
and pleases where it goes.

UNKNOWN AUTHOR

Butterflies © Michael & Patricia Fogden / Minden Pictures

To love and to be loved
is to feel the sun from both sides.

DR. DAVID VISCOTT
American psychiatrist and author

Rhinoceroses © *Joanne Williams*

Love is friendship set on fire.

JEREMY TAYLOR
English bishop and theologian

Giraffes © Jim Brandenburg / Minden Pictures

Our love is like the misty rain
that falls softly—
but floods the river.

AFRICAN PROVERB

Horses © Art Wolfe / PR Inc.net

Your love covers me like a blanket
and keeps me warm.

UNKNOWN AUTHOR

Snow monkeys © Michael L. Peck / Image State, Inc.

True love is the joy of life.

JOHN CLARKE
English clergyman and physician

Indian elephants © Masahiro Iijima / Ardea London

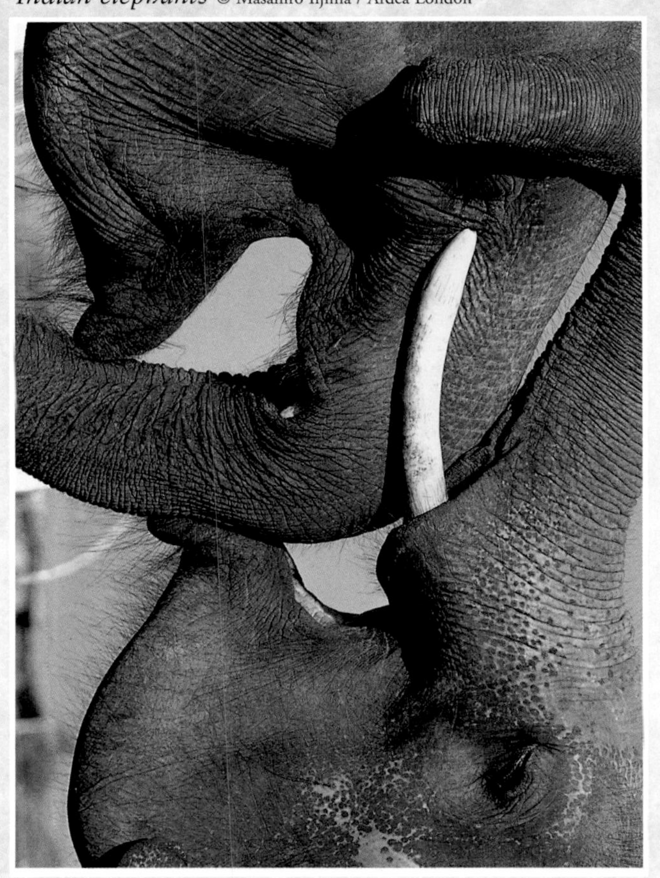

To get the full value of joy
you must have someone
to divide it with.

MARK TWAIN
American writer and humorist

Lemurs © Karl & Kay Amman / BCIUSA

Love flies, runs, and leaps for joy . . .

THOMAS A KEMPIS
Cologne Catholic priest, monk, and writer

Dolphins © Brandon D. Cole

All that is in the heart
is written on the face.

AMISH PROVERB

Orangutans © Daniel J. Cox / Natural Exposures, Inc

There are short-cuts to happiness and dancing is one of them.

VICKI BAUM
Austrian-American novelist

Polar bears © Frans Lanting / Minden Pictures

You have to dance like no one is watching and love like it's never going to hurt.

ANN WELLS
American columnist

Flamingoes © Kirk Yarnell / Super Stock

To love is to be vulnerable.

C.S. Lewis
English literary scholar

Young opossums © Alan and Sandy Carey

Love takes off masks that we fear we cannot live without and know we cannot live within.

JAMES A. BALDWIN
American author

Giraffes © Daniel J. Cox / Natural Exposures, Inc.

Whatever our souls are made of,
his and mine are the same.

EMILY BRONTE
English novelist

Timber wolves © Jim Brandenburg / Minden Pictures

Love . . .
includes fellowship in suffering,
in joy, and in effort.

Dr. Albert Schweitzer
French missionary surgeon

Lions © Anup Shah / Nature Picture Library

Love is an act of endless forgiveness,
a tender look which becomes a habit.

PETER USTINOV
British actor, writer, and director

Swans © Frank Krahmer / BCI USA

To be lucky in love
requires falling in love many times—
and always with the same person.

MIGNON MCLAUGHLIN
American journalist and author

King penguins © Frans Lanting / Minden Pictures

The essence of love is kindness.

ROBERT LOUIS STEVENSON
Scottish author

Timber wolves © Jim Brandenburg / Minden Pictures

*Love is that condition
in which the happiness of another
person is essential to your own.*

ROBERT A. HEINLEIN
American author

King penguins © Frans Lanting / Minden Pictures

My heart is ever at your service.

WILLIAM SHAKESPEARE

Siberian tigers © Tom & Pat Leeson / Leeson Photography

If I had a flower
for every time I thought of you,
I could walk in my garden forever.

ALFRED LORD TENNYSON
English poet

Grizzly bear © Mike & Lisa Husar / Team Husar

I want to do with you
what spring does
with the cherry trees.

PABLO NERUDA
Chilean poet and diplomat

Uinta ground squirrels © Shin Yoshino / Minden Pictures

I love thee like puddings;
if thou wert pie I'd eat thee.

JOHN RAY
English philosopher and theologian

Cheetahs © Mitsuaki Iwago / Minden Pictures

Love is a sweet torment.

THOMAS DRAXE
English writer

Chihuahua puppies © Mitsuaki Iwago / Minden Pictures

Love does not begin and end the way we seem to think it does. Love is a battle, love is a war; love is a growing up.

JAMES A. BALDWIN
American author

Lions © Dale Sweeney / Image State

You're the one
I love to love,
hate to hate,
love to hate, and
hate to love.

Unknown author

Laysan albatross © Frans Lanting / Minden Pictures

The heart has its reasons
which reason knows nothing of.

BLAISE PASCAL
French scientist and religious philosopher

Sandwich terns © Tim Fitzharris / Minden Pictures

The course of true love
never did run smooth.

William Shakespeare

Horned puffins © Gary Schultz / Alaska Stock Images

Let there be spaces in your togetherness.

KAHLIL GIBRAN
Lebanese poet, philosopher, and artist

Cheetahs © Mitsuaki Iwago / Minden Pictures

Honor the ocean of love.

George de Benneville
English physician and lay preacher

Dolphins © Greg Hyuglin / Image State, Inc.

Love does not consist in gazing at each other,
but in looking outward together
in the same direction.

ANTOINE DE SAINT-EXUPERY
French pilot, poet, and author

Lynx © Konrad Wothe / Minden Pictures

Love binds everything together in perfect harmony.

THE BIBLE, COLOSSIANS 3:14

Zebras © Daniel J. Cox / Natural Exposures, Inc.

In love, one and one are one.

JEAN PAUL SARTRE
French novelist and playwright

Red-crowned cranes © Konrad Wothe / Minden Pictures

The entire sum of existence
is the magic of being needed
by just one person.

VI PUTNAM

Polar bears © Mi hael L. Peck / Image State, Inc.

Night and day,
you are the one.

COLE PORTER
American composer

Macaws © Howie Garber / Wanderlust Images

Bibliography

Grateful acknowledgment is made to the authors and publishers for use of the following material. If notified, the publisher will be pleased to rectify an omission in future editions.

Barry, Lynda. *The Good Times are Killing Me*. Seattle, WA: Sasquatch Books, 1999.

Brown, H. Jackson. P.S. *I Love You: When Mom Wrote She Always Saved the Best for Last*. Nashville: Rutledge Hill Press, 1999.

Buchner, Georg. *Leonce and Lena*. 1836. Tanslated by Victor Price. Reprint, Oxford, UK: Oxford University Press, 1999.

Draxe, Thomas. *Bibliotheca scholastica instructissima: Or a Treasure of Ancient Adages*. 1616. Reprint, Norwood, NJ: Walter J. Johnson, Incorporated, 1976.

Fiduccia, Kate [ed.]. *The Quotable Lover*. Guilford, CT: The Lyons Press, 2000.

Fitzhenry, Robert I [ed.]. *The Harper Book of Quotations*, 3rd edition. New York: HarperCollins, 1994.

Frank, Leonard Roy [ed.]. *Random House Webster's Quotationary*. New York: Random House Reference, 1998.

Gibran, Kahlil. *The Prophet*. New York: Alfred A. Knopf, 1923.

Goodman, Ted [ed.]. *The Forbes Book of Business Quotations: Thoughts on the Business of Life*. New York: Black Dog & Leventhal Publishers, 1997.

Heinlein, Robert A. *Stranger in a Strange Land*. New York: G. P. Putnam's Sons, 1961.

Heller, Elizabeth. *Little Lessons of Love*. Berkeley, CA: Conari Press, 1995.

a Kempis, Thomas. *The Imitation of Christ.* 1418. Translated by Leo Sherly-Price. Reprint, New York: Viking Press, 1952.

Lewis, C.S. *The Pattern of Pain.* San Francisco: Harper San Francisco, 2002.

Linfield, Jordon L. [ed.], et al. *Words of Love: Romantic Quotations from Plato to Madonna.* New York: Gramercy Books, 1998.

Neruda, Pablo. "Every Day You Play" [1924]. *Pablo Neruda: Selected Poems,* Bilingual Edition. Translated by Anthony Kerrigan. Boston: Mariner Books, 1990.

Proust, Marcel. *The Guermantes Way.* 1921. Reprint, New York: Random House, 1981.

Quinn, Tracy [ed.]. *Quotable Women of the Twentieth Century.* New York: William Morrow & Co., 1999.

Simpson, James B. [compiled by]. *Simpson's Contemporary Quotations.* Boston: Houghton Mifflin, 1988.

Schweitzer, Albert. *The Philosophy of Civilization: Civilization and Ethics,* 3rd ed. Translated by C. T. Campion. Revised by Mrs. Charles E. B. Russell. Reprint, London: A. & C. Black, 1946.

Ustinov, Peter. *Christian Science Monitor.* Boston: 9 Dec 1958.

Viscott, David. *How to Live with Another Person.* New York: Pocket Books, 1983.

Wells, Ann. "What are You Waiting For?" *Los Angeles Times,* 14 April 1985.

Wyatt, Woodrow. "To the Point." *London Sunday Times.* 22 March 1981.

Zona, Guy A. *True Love is Friendship Set on Fire.* New York: Touchstone Books, 1998.

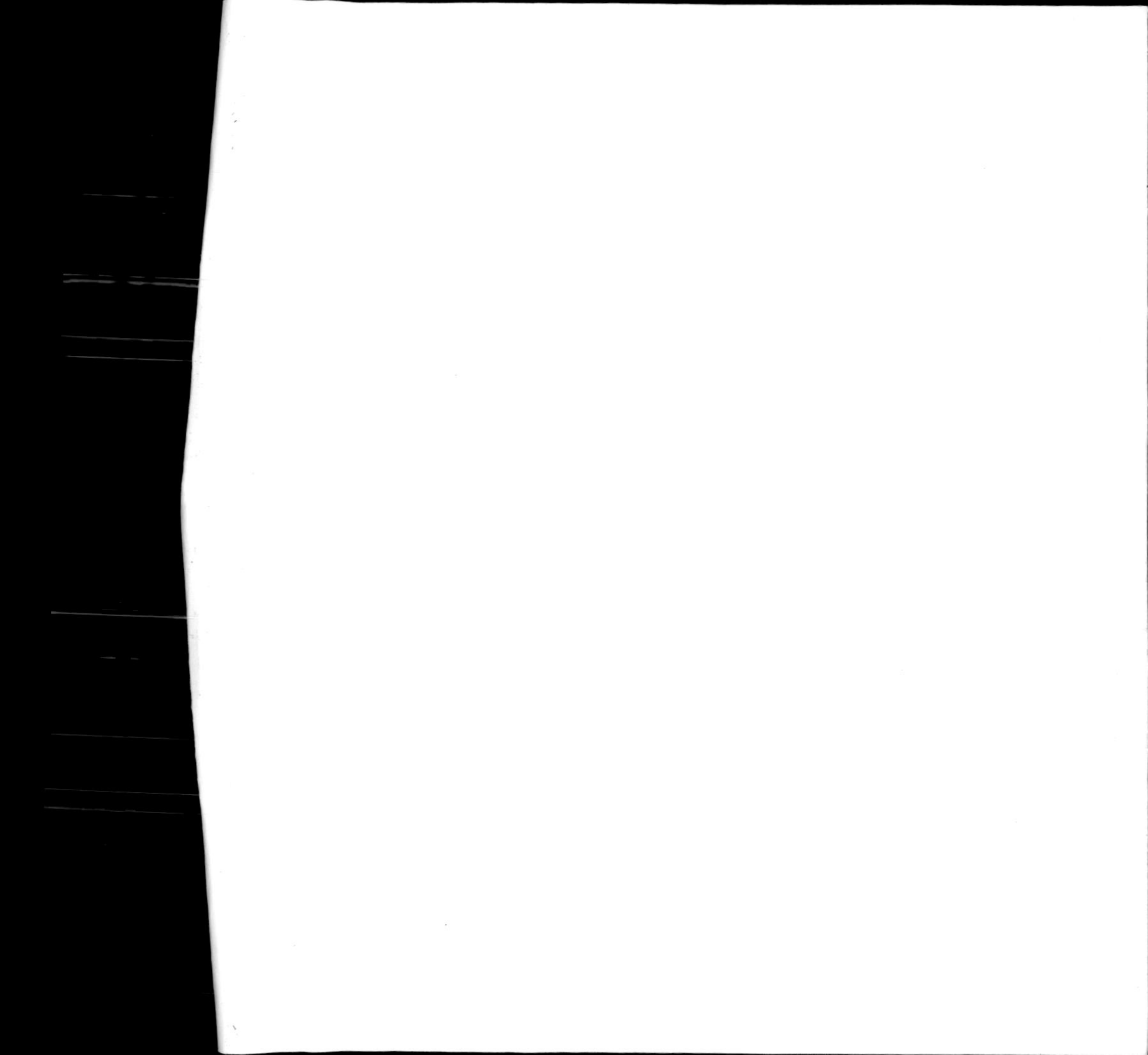